T0208853

THE
KUNDALINI REIKI
MANUAL

A Guide for Kundalini Reiki Attuners and Clients

LISA OKOCHI

THE KUNDALINI REIKI MANUAL
A Guide for Kundalini Reiki Attuners and Clients

iUniverse books may be ordered through booksellers or by contacting:

iUniverse
1663 Liberty Drive
Bloomington, IN 47403
www.iuniverse.com
1-800-Authors (1-800-288-4677)

ISBN: 978-1-4917-7744-2 (sc)
ISBN: 978-1-4917-7745-9 (e)

Print information available on the last page.

iUniverse rev. date: 01/12/2017

"Your Kundalini energy is the fuel from the Earth that grounds you and the synergy with Reiki, which is soft and loving, reconnects you to your Higher Self. It is the key to Joy."

—Ole Gabrielsen
Founder, Kundalini Reiki

Dedicated to Ole Gabrielsen

With special gratitude to my teachers:
Meltem Oner
Raphael Legros
—for passing on the gift of Kundalini Reiki teaching

And to Marilyn Horowitz for her amazing
advice and Loraine Jones for her support!

DISCLAIMER

Natural healing techniques are a complement and not a substitute for any professional medical diagnosis.

Natural healers and holistic therapists do not diagnose conditions or prescribe medical treatments.

Please consult your physician or health-care specialist, prior to Reiki treatment, if you have any health concerns.

Reiki healers are not responsible for clients who decide to change or stop their medications or medical treatments.

It is recommended that the minimum age for an attunement be eight years old, with consent from parents or legal guardian and a duration of not longer than 5 to10 minutes.

—Lisa Okochi, lead organizer, U.S.A.

TABLE OF
CONTENTS

INTRODUCTION.. i

CHAPTER 1 1
A History of Reiki and the Kundalini

CHAPTER 2 4
What Are the Necessary Steps to
Becoming a K.R. Practitioner?

CHAPTER 3 9
Kundalini Reiki Level 1 Attunement

CHAPTER 4 18
Kundalini Reiki 2 Attunement

CHAPTER 5 21
Kundalini Reiki Level 3 Attunement

CHAPTER 6 32
For Clients: Important Notes to Remember

CHAPTER 7 34
For Kundalini Reiki Practitioners

CHAPTER 8 40
Gold Reiki Attunements, Levels 1–3

CHAPTER 9 45
Ethereal Crystal Reiki Attunements, Levels 1–9

CHAPTER 10 58
How to Heal and Attune Remotely: An Overview

CHAPTER 11 62
Reiki Clinic for the Community

CONCLUSION 65
QUICK REFERENCE GUIDE 67
SUGGESTED READING 68
ABOUT THE AUTHOR 69

INTRODUCTION

Kundalini Reiki is a new 21st century self-healing system that takes an ancient Japanese healing art and integrates it with a modern holistic technique to fulfill the needs of those of us who have lost touch with our true selves and are searching for answers outside the range of medical science.

This introductory manual is meant for K.R. practitioners and anyone searching for new, simple, and alternative self-healing techniques for chronic physical and mental stress. This is the first and only healing system that has the potential to dissipate birth trauma, genetic issues, chronic pain, and negative past-life residues, to name a few—all in one easy five-minute practice. This manual will help clients prepare for and understand what K.R. is, how to be attuned," and why it can effectively change your life. Attunements are spiritual activations of your energetic fields. Each attunement systematically upgrades and programs your body to receive higher frequencies of Reiki energy. (Please note: you need to be attuned by a Kundalini Reiki Certified Master in order to use these practices on yourself and others. Master healers of other energy work also need to be attuned.)

K.R. is for people of all beliefs and walks of life!

From an early age, I have always been fascinated with crystals and the healing arts. I have been blessed to study with several powerful mentors over the years, acquiring knowledge and experience in many healing modalities both here and in Japan, such as Pranic Healing, reflexology, meditation, yoga, massage, and traditional Reiki. So, as a healer for many years myself, I could not believe it could be so simple.

I come from a generation of healers. I remember when I was a child in Japan, if I cut myself, my late grandmother would chant, then blow on the cut three times. Although I don't remember if the pain went away any faster this way, my mother told me years later that people from all over the village would come to my grandmother to be healed. All she did was chant the same words and then blow three time on the painful area. My mother distinctly recalls a girlfriend of hers coming with a severe earache, and that the chant made it disappear right away.

Apparently, when my grandmother was a young girl, a Buddhist high priest passed the chant on to her, commanding her to heal others with it. She helped many during World War II, when medical doctors were scarce. My great grandfather was a Japanese priest whom my mother remembers often predicting illnesses and death of villagers. My mother also has natural abilities to heal, although she does not practice the chants. My grandmother never had a chance to pass on her knowledge as I grew up in the west and had passed away by the time my family returned to Japan. But my spiritual fascination continued to grow, and I had to study several types of energy work at multiple centers, attend retreats in temples to chant, sit under icy waterfalls, and be initiated to receive various certifications over the years in order to finally get in touch with this amazing refined energy source suitable for the 21st century.

This manual will provide simple, easy-to-follow explanations of Reiki and the Kundalini and how the two practices, when combined, create a powerful energy source. It will explain the difference between a healing and an attunement and how together you can regain control of your life. It is the first healing system where you no longer need to be passively receiving from or depending on healing therapists.

It is also a different type of frequency than traditional Reiki, which will be clarified in Chapter 2. We now have a completely updated 21st-century version, which is slowly spreading internationally and may likely replace the older system. K.R. is purer and hence more powerful. It is a highly effective and simple self-healing tool kit that absolutely anyone can use at home and in our modern, on-the-go lifestyle. It has immense practical and beneficial value to help you regain control of your emotions; restore your focus, health, and inner peace; reconnect you to your spirit and identity; and reconnect to others from your heart.

The biggest difference from other healing arts is that, in this case, not only do you receive the Reiki energy quickly, safely, and permanently, you also can easily attune others, using the tools to heal your own issues as well as those of loved ones—or even a stranger in an emergency!

K.R. is like a high-speed version of Reiki that, for the first time, does not require intensive training, although it does require supervision by an advanced K.R. practitioner. It is a safe, simple technique that is meant to be shared with the world. It is for anyone who wants to learn how to be more self-sufficient, joyful, less stressed, and healthier in mind, body, and soul. And it is for those who want to feel empowered to help themselves and their families.

K.R. is not meant to replace other practices or belief systems. It is a practical, adaptable energy that can be integrated into anyone's lifestyle.

We are living in troubled times of social and emotional upheaval that have created a whole new level of physical, mental, and financial issues, which most of us cannot keep pace with. Too often we live in fear of speaking our truths, instead covering them up with anger, overeating, addictions, and we don't know how to change. There has been a significant increase in interest in alternative modalities, which are less invasive, less costly, and safer than traditional bio-medical approaches. Science and holistic therapies are coming together to acknowledge that everything in nature is made of vibrational energy: in other words every place person, thing, and emotion in your life influences your own vibrational well-being or "vibes," if you will. If that is so, and I believe it is, then the outer fields of each vibration will inevitably affect and mingle with other energetic fields around them.

Therefore, it is in our best interest to search for and develop a regular practice to harmonize, clear, and realign energy blockages that occur in our body and minds.

This manual will guide you through the preparations and expectations of each attunement-level workshop. There are essentially three series, each one containing three levels: Kundalini Reiki, Gold Reiki, and Ethereal Crystal Reiki. The completion of all three levels will upgrade your vibrational frequency and grant you a certification without exams. For best results, it is suggested that you aim to complete one series at a time over three weeks. Each level should take approximately one to two hours, with the actual attunement taking approximately 25 minutes. Practicing the easy exercises will make Kundalini Reiki second nature to you. But above all, we ask that you enjoy it. This is a gift from God.

CHAPTER 1

A History of Reiki and the Kundalini

"Reiki" is the Japanese word for spiritual energy. "Rei" is spirit, the ethereal, while "Ki" connotes life-force energy. Reiki is a frequency. It is the energy that flows through all living beings. The word uses the same Chinese characters as the "Qi" in Qigong and the "Chi" in Tai Chi. In science, all matter, animate and inanimate, is made up of vibrational frequencies. Reiki is a high, subtle vibration that helps revitalize and re-align imbalances in our body, mind, and soul.

Many of us might have heard of, or already practice, traditional Reiki, called "Usui." It originated in Japan in the 1870s. Meditating on a holy mountain, Mikao Usui, a monk and doctor, felt a huge surge of energy flowing down over his head, which miraculously healed his ailments. He realized he had been gifted with this energy pouring down his crown chakra to his hands. He called this powerful energy "Reiki" and passed on the Usui energy technique to thousands. As Usui felt his whole lifestyle shift, he added spiritual teachings and symbolism to create a Reiki system. This Usui Reiki system was very popular in the '70s. Trainings were and still are intense, long-term, costly, and involve initiations, sacred symbols, and mastering the art of laying hands on or slightly above patients to channel the Reiki to heal them.

K.R., however, takes the same principles and adapts them to our present-day needs.

The term "Kundalini" is often misunderstood, but when the technique is applied properly, it is one of the strongest energy sources in our being, one that lies "sleeping" at the base of our spine, just waiting to be roused. For us to achieve total enlightenment, we have to "wake it up." It is often depicted mythically, as a double serpent, emphasizing that its activation is by no means an easy task, usually requiring years of solitary meditation. In fact, stimulating it without proper guidance can actually be dangerous. You should never experiment with this energy without supervision. In practice, the Kundalini energy is located in the base of our spine in our base chakra and is more like a fuel tank that recharges from the Earth's core energy and prana to help sustain our vitality, health, and focus. It holds the force of our body, mind, and spirit and our connection to Mother Earth. As long as the Kundalini remains inactive, it is difficult to stay "grounded" in our competitive society. The problem is that most of the world's population is unaware of this power we have stored within us and that it has the potential to change our life in so many ways.

Kundalini Reiki

This new K.R. technique, however, combines and safely harnesses the raw energy of the Kundalini and turns it into a healing force. It's an incredibly easy, fast way to combine Reiki with the "Kundalini Fire." No more secret symbols or rituals are involved.

The School of Kundalini Reiki was founded by Ole Gabrielsen, a powerful, renowned meditator and healer. He became gifted with this new energy through holy communion with the spiritual universe in deep meditation. Ole was trying to find a way to combine Reiki with Kundalini activation when he received guided messages from Ascended Master Kuthumi, who revealed the steps to create Kundalini Reiki. Ascended Masters are based on the belief that highly evolved humans who once walked the Earth are now spiritual Masters assisting the world from higher realms, with their wisdom, love, and peace. Lord Jesus, Moses, Mother Mary, Lord Buddha, and Yogananda are to name a few. Ole then tapped into the energetic frequency of this Reiki directly from Source, the Creator, bypassing Usui to activate the Kundalini safely.

Ever since his revelation, Ole Gabrielsen has been traveling all over the world to attune countless people. They, in turn, have been passing on the Reiki attunements to others. Once you are attuned, you can attune yourself very easily following the simple system. He believes it is time to get away from intellectual arrogance and start focusing on healing the physical body and mind through the safe activation of our Kundalini with the loving energy of Source Reiki, which holds the key to light and joy.

CHAPTER 2

What Are the Necessary Steps to Becoming a K.R. Practitioner?

In this chapter, you will learn what you need to know to prepare for the K.R. attunements and the steps to becoming a K.R. practitioner. There are four main steps:

1. First find a certified K.R. practitioner who conducts private or class sessions to be attuned to each level. Please go online to kundalinireiki.org, "Kundalini Reiki NYC" on Facebook. It is also possible to receive attunements remotely if you cannot find a practitioner near you.
2. Practice with the tools using only one short meditation technique. You will be taught various tools to heal certain areas in your life with supervision.
3. Self-heal. Continue to work on healing yourself with the powerful tools.
4. Attune/heal others. You will then be guided to safely and properly attune and heal others.

When you find a K.R. practitioner, commit to three sessions; one session per week. Each level is important in preparing you to fully awaken your Kundalini in Level 3. You cannot skip a level or feel the effectiveness with just one level. Even Grand Masters of traditional Usui Reiki cannot forgo a level. It is also possible to receive attunements remotely if you cannot find a practitioner near you.

What Is an Attunement?

The goal of all Reiki practitioners is to be attuned to this new version no matter how advanced the healer is. An "attunement" is a procedure whereby a person (or spirit guide) passes on a specific energy structure to another person's (receiver's) energy and/or energy centers (chakras). This enables the receiver to become a permanent channel for that specific energy. When we talk of energy centers, chakras, or vibes, we are really referring to the biochemical and bioelectrical systems in our bodies. The K.R. essentially clears your chakras to prepare your Kundalini to be safely activated from the base of your spine.

Chakras are energy centers in your body that control certain organs, body parts, and emotions. They are governed by the endocrine system. Details will be given for each Reiki level.

In order to practice K.R., you need to tap into this spiritual frequency through an attunement to the Source, via Ascended Master Kuthumi, spiritual guides, and a K.R. practitioner.

It is very much like wireless technology. If you want to use Wi-Fi for Internet service, you need to switch on the wireless button on your device, choose a network, and log on. Only then do you have access to the wealth of information online. But do we really need to know and understand the science behind how it works? No. Most of us don't care, as long as it works. From a spiritual perspective, this is similar to the K.R. attunement system. The K.R. Master will channel the different levels of Reiki energy into the receiver safely, simply, and quickly.

What Is the Purpose of the Invocation?

Each time you want to be attuned or practice, you need to ask for or "invoke" spiritual assistance to contact the Reiki. It is strongly suggested you invoke for any universal power—any Ascended Masters, angels, and/or guides you believe in—to assist you and to call forth Ascended Master Kuthumi to honor and respect the Source. It will empower the Reiki.

Once you are attuned to a level, the K.R. energy is permanently part of your system and you can use the healing energy in your practices. Each level will increase your ability to heal various issues and give you new tools to practice with.

Preparations

1. If you are not in a class, find a quiet space where you will not be disturbed for 30 minutes and turn off your cell phone. You may play calming music on a stereo, but do not wear headphones.
2. Sit in a comfortable position with palms facing upwards on your lap and legs flat on the floor. You may also lie down with your palms facing upwards. Do not cross your legs. This will allow for the Reiki to flow to your hand and feet chakras.

3. Touch the tip of your tongue to the roof of your mouth, center yourself with your breath, take three deep inhales into your heart, and exhale slowly. Take three breaths into your stomach to relax tension. Then invoke to your higher self and any guides or angels you believe in to ask for assistance and for the White Light of Protection to surround you. In your heart say, "Please attune me to Kundalini Reiki Level [here name the level number]."

4. Relax and allow the K.R. practitioner to let the energy flow through you.

The K.R. practitioner will "connect" you. It takes approximately 25 minutes for the K.R. Master to "download" the K.R. frequency into your energy field. All you need to do during the attunement is relax. If you're in a private session, the K.R. Master will either sit near you or place his or her hands lightly on your shoulders. It's all right to fall asleep. Don't try to think too hard. Once you receive the energy, you can practice with the tools anytime, anywhere. You will have the ability to heal whole groups in just a few minutes! No intense focus or hands-on work is necessary. The flow of Reiki will go where you intend it. It is the Law of Attraction.

The Practice

1. After an attunement, decide what you would like to heal and simply write it on your hand with your finger. You can also write it on a piece of paper or even envision the issue and yourself as a "mini me" in your hand.

2. Put your palms together with all fingers touching, as if you are cupping the issue. (You may know this

as prayer position, not pressing the palms closed. Please see the book-cover photo, if necessary.)

3. Invoke for your spiritual guides and/or angels you believe in and say "Reiki." The Reiki will flow into your hands and send healing energy into whatever you wrote down or envisioned.

Take approximately three to five minutes before releasing the hand position.

The practices are mini meditations and are meant to be simple and easy to follow. Although you will have some abilities to heal, it is not until you complete K.R. Level 3 that the Kundalini will be fully awakened and you will be grounded to the Earth Source and the universe. You will be certified to attune others after Level 3 under the supervision of your practitioner until such time that you feel confident to perform the practice on your own.

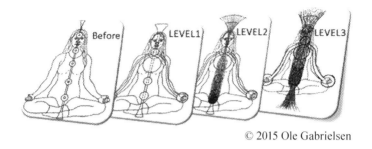

CHAPTER 3

Kundalini Reiki Level 1 Attunement

This chapter will help you understand what will happen when the first level of Reiki frequency is transferred into your energy field by the K.R. practitioner.

The 1st Attunement will focus on clearing all the blockages in your energy centers (chakras) except for the root chakra. Level 1 will open and widen your crown center, heart, and hand chakras. This is important because the Reiki pathway flows through the crown into your heart and hands to help you heal yourself and others. Therefore, it is important that your hand centers are opened.

Chakras are energy centers in the body that control various organs, body parts, and emotions. Clearing the chakra system alone can make you feel considerably better.

Preparations

1. If you are not in a class, find a quiet space where you will not be disturbed for 30 minutes and turn off your cell phone. You may play calming music on a stereo, but do not wear headphones.
2. Sit in a comfortable position with palms facing upwards on your lap and legs flat on the floor. You may also lie down with your palms facing upwards. Do not cross your legs. This will allow for the Reiki to flow to your hand and feet chakras.
3. Touch the tip of your tongue to the roof of your mouth, center yourself with your breath, take three deep inhales into your heart, and exhale slowly. Take three breaths into your stomach to relax tension. Then invoke to your higher self, Master Kuthumi, and any guides or angels you believe in to ask for assistance and for the White Light of Protection to

surround you. In your heart say, "Please attune me to Kundalini Reiki Level 1."

4. Relax and allow the attuner to let the energy flow through you.

As the Kundalini Reiki Master is channeling Reiki 1 into your energy field, you may feel heat, trembling, vibrations, see colors, even have flashes of visions as you receive. This is due to the Reiki drawing out the blockages.

Every individual will experience exactly what they need or are ready for. Reiki will give you just the right amount necessary for you. I have yet to have a client who didn't feel or experience anything.

After the 25-minute attunement, you might feel lighter and more focused. At this point you will be given some specific tools and abilities to heal certain issues.

Healing Abilities After the Kundalini Reiki Level 1 Attunement

After Level 1, you can practice healing issues regarding your health, negative emotions, situations, karmic cords, and places of negative energy. Each practice gives you a tool, but the technique for every tool will be the same.

How to Heal Yourself and Others: The Practice

Prepare: Sit quietly, upright, with feet planted on the floor. Touch the tip of your tongue to the roof of your mouth and start to focus on breathing deeply and evenly. Do this a few times to ground and center yourself. Then close your eyes and ask for the White Light of Protection to surround you as you call to your higher self and guides for assistance.

The first tool will be to help you disconnect from certain people and situations by cutting the "Karmic cords."

What Are Karmic Cords?

When we are in a relationship, there are spiritual cords that connect us to each other, especially between our hearts. The longer we are together, the stronger the cord. That is why we feel so depressed or can't let go of someone after we break up.

To cut that connecting spiritual cord, simply write the person's name in the palm of one hand with your finger. You can also write it on a piece of paper or envision the person and yourself as a mini me in your hand.

Put your palms together with all fingers touching, as if you are cupping the issue.

Invoke for your spiritual guides and/or angels, Ascended Master Kuthumi, and say, "Cut the cords between me and [name of person]. Reiki!" The Reiki will flow from your hands into the wish you wrote or envisioned.

Take approximately three to five minutes before releasing the hand position. Do this practice as often as needed and have faith that it is so.

If you are suffering from a stressful situation, you can also, using the same technique, replace a person with the situation you want to detach from.

The next tool will help you detach from unwanted feelings such as anger, envy, and sadness by using the same technique. Emotions are energy. Reiki can help dissipate negative ones that you can't seem let go of.

How to Let Go of Negative Emotions

Prepare: Sit quietly, upright, with feet planted on the floor. Touch the tip of your tongue to the roof of your mouth and start to focus on breathing deeply and evenly. Do this a few times to ground and center yourself. Then close your eyes and ask for the White Light of Protection to surround you as you call to your higher self and guides for assistance.

For example, if you have anger issues, write "my anger" or "my anger against [name here]" in your palm. Close your hands in prayer position and say "Reiki!" Visualize the Reiki flowing through your hands and dissipating the emotion.

If you are going through a troubled relationship with a partner, co-worker, or friend, write "My Relationship with _____," and say "Reiki!" Do not worry if you said or wrote the words correctly as the Reiki will know how to help you.

Release your hands after three to five minutes. The Reiki will continue to flow a while longer.

Repeat this as often as needed and you will notice a shift over time. Either you will start to stand up for yourself more definitively or the other person might start initiating a separation. It's also possible that a situation will arise that removes the other person to another location.

The following tool will assist you in relieving physical discomfort but is not meant to replace medical treatment. Instead, it can speed up recovery if medication is also needed. Also note that there are different levels of pain. If there are deep psychological scars, you will need to address the pain with various tools of Reiki and supervision from other professional fields.

How to Heal Pain Issues

Prepare: Sit quietly, upright, with feet planted on the floor. Touch the tip of your tongue to the roof of your mouth and start to focus on breathing deeply and evenly. Do this a few times to ground and center yourself. Then close your eyes and ask for the White Light of Protection to surround you as you call to your higher self and guides for assistance.

For example, if you have a headache, write "my headache" into your palm with a finger and visualize yourself in your hand. Then cup your palms together in prayer position and invoke by saying "Reiki" and relax. Allow the Reiki to flow through your hands to the topic.

You do not need to focus hard. The intention will go out there. Just relax and feel how your body is reacting.

In three to five minutes, release your hands. The Reiki will continue to flow for a while afterward. Feeling heat in your hands is a clear sign that it is working. If, however, you know the headache is coming from anger towards someone or some situation, you will need to address that anger and the relationship with Reiki as well.

The next tool is very useful when you feel your room, office, or even a public place is stuffy or stale. Just as we vacuum and clean up dirt and dust in our home, we need to clean the energy in our home and workplace as they accumulate energy from everyone's thoughts and words. Some of you might be sensitive and feel negative vibes in a place. Clearing the space with Reiki is a powerful tool.

How to Clear Negative Energy in a Space

Prepare: Sit quietly, upright, with feet planted on the floor. Touch the tip of your tongue to the roof of your mouth

14

and start to focus on breathing deeply and evenly. Do this a few times to ground and center yourself. Then close your eyes and ask for the White Light of Protection to surround you as you call to your higher self and guides for assistance.

Write or visualize "my home" or "my office" in your hands, invoke, and say "Reiki." After three to five minutes, release your hands. The Reiki will continue to flow for a while afterward. It is recommended to perform this practice every 14 days, especially if you work in a hospital or negative environment.

Please enjoy the process with these tools. The more you repeat them, the more the Reiki is going to help you. Try to notice how people start seeming kinder around you, too.

Healing Others Individually, in a Group, or Remotely

Sending healing to someone who is in either the same room or in another location follows the exact same preparations as the practice for yourself. If the client is with you, you can place your hands slightly above his or her shoulders and invoke. If he or she is not there, simply do the hand technique. You can send Reiki to any part of the world instantly! I have remotely sent many K.R. attunements and healings internationally with amazing feedback.

Prepare: Sit quietly, upright, with feet planted on the floor. Touch the tip of your tongue to the roof of your mouth and start to focus on breathing deeply and evenly. Do this a few times to ground and center yourself. Then close your eyes and ask for the White Light of Protection to surround you as you call to your higher self and guides for assistance.

For example, Tom Smith has a backache. Write "Tom's backache" in your hand and visualize a mini Tom. Cup the image in a prayer pose, ask your higher self and Master Kuthumi (and whoever you believe in) to send Tom Smith Reiki for his headache. Then invoke by saying "Reiki." If Tom is in a different location, be sure to state his address and full name to make sure that it reaches the right Tom!

If you want to send peace to a tense group of people— say, in your office—write "peace," visualize the group in your hands, and invoke "Reiki!" You will notice the group will seem calmer after not too long.

What if you are trying to help a stranger in an emergency? Well, first ask for permission, if possible. Otherwise follow your heart's innermost conviction and proceed accordingly.

Note: out of respect to others, it is recommended to ask for their permission beforehand. There are some who will not want what you are offering.

Allow About Five Days Between Attunements

The completion of the first attunement will enable you to start practicing self-healing, helping others, and to sooth difficult situations to make your life easier.

Case Studies

Client D.B. returned home after Level 1, and that night she used the Reiki tool to help her husband, who suffers from insomnia. She wrote "My husband's insomnia" in her hands and invoked "Reiki!" After an only five-minute practice, he woke up the next day saying that he hadn't slept so deeply and peacefully in a long time.

On another occasion, I was at a dance when someone I knew started to have an asthma attack and had no medicine with him. After asking his permission, I tried traditional Reiki. After 30 minutes he said he felt better but not well enough to breathe easily. He refused to go to the E.R., so I took him to a quiet place and asked him if he would allow me to perform a new type of Reiki on him. At this point, he was tensely gripping the table, finding it a struggle to breathe. I did a solid five minutes of K.R. practice. My hands got very hot, and I noticed his shoulders and hands start to relax. Soon he had regained his normal breathing. After resting for another 10 minutes, he said he was well enough to go back to dancing, which he did! He later told me that, in these circumstances, he usually ends up in the E.R.

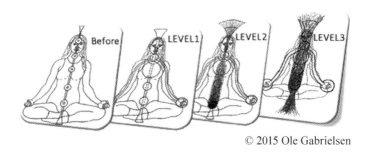

CHAPTER 4

Kundalini Reiki 2 Attunement

This chapter will explain how the K.R. Level 2 Attunement will continue to clear blockages and prepare your body for the Kundalini energy to awaken safely in Level 3.

The Kundalini Reiki Level 2 Attunement is going to clear the final blockage in the root (base) chakra, where the Kundalini energy lies dormant. It will widen your third eye and strengthen Reiki 1. Your Kundalini will rise to the solar-plexus chakra to prepare you for its full awakening in Reiki 3.

Preparations

1. If you are not in a class, find a quiet space where you will not be disturbed for 30 minutes and turn off your cell phone. You may play calming music on a stereo, but do not wear headphones.
2. Sit in a comfortable position with palms facing upwards on your lap and legs flat on the floor. You

may also lie down with your palms facing upwards. Do not cross your legs. This will allow for the Reiki to flow to your hand and feet chakras.

3. Touch the tip of your tongue to the roof of your mouth, center yourself with your breath, take three deep inhales into your heart, and exhale slowly. Take three breaths into your stomach to relax tension. Then invoke to your higher self and any guides or angels you believe in to ask for assistance and for the White Light of Protection to surround you. In your heart say, "Please attune me to Kundalini Reiki Level 2."

4. Relax and allow the practitioner to let the energy flow through you.

The K.R. practitioner will connect you to the Reiki. It takes approximately 25 minutes for the K.R. Master to "download" the K.R. frequency into your energy field. All you need to do during the attunement is relax. If it is a private session, the K.R. Master will either sit near you or place his or her hands lightly on your shoulders. It is all right to fall asleep. Do not try to think too hard.

You may experience some stomach discomfort or a sense of feeling full. You also might see gray or black swirls, feel tingling, and, afterward, notice a lightness or heaviness.

Note: Each Reiki attunement is cleansing and clearing your energy field, so there might be periods of detoxing physically as your body adjusts to the Reiki. Some do feel stomach discomfort following Kundalini Reiki 2 and all the way to Kundalini Reiki 3. This is the Kundalini hanging out, waiting to wake up! To mitigate the problem, practice the Kundalini Reiki meditation daily until the discomfort stops.

Now that you are attuned to K.R. Level 2, you can continue to practice the exercises for K.R. 1 and one new tool for invoking Kundalini Reiki—instead of Reiki—to make the energy stronger.

The Practice After the K.R. Level 2 Attunement

In order to prepare for the Kundalini to fully open in Reiki 3, you are advised to practice the Kundalini meditation as many times as you need to, between Reiki 2 and 3. This meditation will help keep your energy centers clear so your Kundalini has a smooth pathway to flow up.

Kundalini Reiki Meditation Technique

Sit or lie down in quiet place. Put your hands in prayer position. Invoke for your spiritual guide's assistance and say, "Kundalini Reiki meditation." Allow your body to relax and let go of any stress. Visualize the Reiki energy vacuuming out any blockages through your crown chakra. The process will automatically stop after 5 to 15 minutes. You do not need to keep your palms together longer than five minutes.

When you do this, the Kundalini Fire will temporarily light up and cleanse your energy channels (chakras). This is extremely useful, and even those who struggle in their meditation will find it easy. Continue to invoke for Kundalini Reiki instead of Reiki when practicing the exercises in Reiki Level 1.

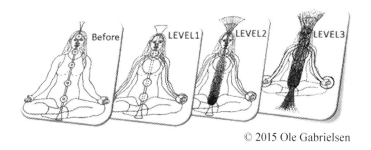

CHAPTER 5

Kundalini Reiki Level 3 Attunement

This chapter will explain what chakras are in more detail and how they expand and allow the flow of your Kundalini energy to rise through your system to reconnect you to your higher self and the universe. I have found this attunement to be the most powerful, based on many clients' experiences both during and after it.

This level will fully and safely activate the Kundalini Life Force in your body. It will widen your throat chakra, solar-plexus chakra, Hara chakra, and base chakra to awaken your spirit, reminding you why you are here and grounding you to your life's purpose.

Chakras help maintain the physical state of our bodies by feeding it Pranic life force or "Ii" (Rei-*ki*) from the ethereal world. Although there are many chakras, we have seven major ones, and each controls certain regions, organs, and emotions.

For example, the third eye is governed by the pituitary gland, the master hormone center, which stores your intuition and focus in life and controls the endocrine system.

The throat chakra represents creativity and communicating your truth. It is governed by the thyroid and holds the general health of your neck. It can get blocked up by trauma or an unsupportive loved one, which in turn can create chronic throat issues or pain.

If you are one to "swallow" your words or "crush your creative talents," you might eventually develop blockages in your throat chakra to the point of having thyroid issues.

The solar plexus is about willpower and confidence. When it gets blocked with frustration or stress, it can result in physical symptoms like acid reflux or stomach ulcers.

The Hara ("stomach" in Japanese) is a powerful center below the naval that stores Ki energy. It is the central force martial artists draw from to chop bricks in half with their feet or hands.

The base chakra holds your power to survive spiritually, emotionally, and financially. It stores your ability to be successful and have abundance. Fear or anger can block this center and create depression, sluggishness, and leg issues. A strong base chakra will empower you as you strengthen the Kundalini Life Force in this area.

Kundalini Reiki Levels 1 and 2 prepare you to safely allow the Kundalini energy to rise up the body to your crown chakra to reconnect you to your higher soul. The crown chakra channel can now open to allow the right information from higher realms to flow down to assist you on your journey.

Preparations

1. If you are not in a class, find a quiet space where you will not be disturbed for 30 minutes and turn off your cell phone. You may play calming music on a stereo, but do not wear headphones.
2. Sit in a comfortable position with palms facing upwards on your lap and legs flat on the floor. You may also lie down with your palms facing upwards. Do not cross your legs. This will allow for the Reiki to flow to your hand and feet chakras.
3. Touch the tip of your tongue to the roof of your mouth, center yourself with your breath, take three deep inhales into your heart, and exhale slowly. Take three breaths into your stomach to relax tension. Then invoke to your higher self and any guides or angels you believe in to ask for assistance and for the White Light of Protection to surround you. In your heart say, "Please attune me to Kundalini Reiki Level 3."
4. Relax and allow the K.R. practitioner to channel the energy into your energy field.

The K.R. practitioner will connect you to the Reiki. It takes approximately 25 minutes for the K.R. Master to "download" the K.R. frequency into your energy field. All you need to do during the attunement is relax. If it is a private session, the K.R. Master will either sit near you or place his or her hands lightly on your shoulders. It is all right to fall asleep. Do not try to think too hard.

What You May Experience During an Attunement

Recipients commonly feel strong vibrational tingling—especially in the hands and feet—heat, sensations of energy moving either towards the feet or head. They may also see colors and, sometimes, flashes of visions. Remember, the K.R. practitioner will always create a safe environment so that you feel secure during your attunement.

Note: I've recognized a clear difference between those who practice the Kundalini meditations and Reiki exercises and those who do not. Those who do practice feel lighter afterward, while those who don't practice are prone to lethargy and sleepiness for a few days. This is a sign of detox. It may also happen if you have been on a long-term medication. Do not be discouraged. Practice the exercises and invoke for energy. Eventually your body will adjust to the high frequency and calm down.

The Practice After Kundalini Reiki Level 3

The following Reiki techniques may seem "out there" to many people, but I ask that you keep an open mind. The tools in this level have the potential to address issues in your life that you may not have conceived connections to before.

In this third attunement, an Ethereal Diamond will be placed over your crown chakra. This means that each time you invoke, the Reiki will flow through this "spiritual" diamond, which adds more power to your tools and practice. The diamond's pure qualities will strengthen your energy to heal. So, when you practice with the tools from any level, you may now invoke for "Diamond Reiki" instead of "Kundalini

Reiki." For example, if you are feeling tense, you can invoke and ask for your tension to ease and say, "Diamond Reiki." Do not worry whether you use the right Reiki, because your intentions will still send Reiki.

After the K.R. Level 3 Attunement, the first thing you can do is heal any issues you might have had at birth or during pregnancy that still affect you now, whether or not you are aware of them.

Birth Trauma Reiki

What if you had a difficult birth that affects you to this day, whether it's an emotional trait like anxiety, fear of the dark, or a bad neck? We might not recall our birth, but memory cells can hold on to it. So, why not "Reiki erase" it? Have faith.

Prepare: Sit quietly, upright, with feet planted on the floor. Touch the tip of your tongue to the roof of your mouth and focus on breathing deeply and evenly. Do this a few times to ground and center yourself. Then close your eyes and ask for the White Light of Protection to surround you as you call to your higher self and guides for assistance.

Write or visualize the words "My birth trauma" in your palm. For example, if you know you have a specific trauma related to your birth, write "My birth trauma for panic." Close your hands in prayer position and invoke for "birth-trauma Reiki" for three to five minutes. Imagine the Reiki flowing back to your time of birth and dissipating any traumatic residues. Once is enough unless you feel you need to address it more.

We do not really know the extent of damage that pollution, ozone holes, power lines, and genetically modified products can have on our DNA over time. So even if you are not aware of any inherited genetic diseases, like Parkinson's, it is recommended to perform the DNA Reiki practice.

DNA Reiki

This Reiki has the potential to help realign your DNA strands. It is said that results may be noticed after three weeks. I suggest you do this to cover all your bases, even if you find it requires a leap of faith. Please practice this if you or a loved one is suffering from a genetic disease, and do your own empirical study. I once attuned an artist with Parkinson's to K.R. and Gold Reiki. At the time, his symptoms were rapidly progressing. Although he wasn't sure it helped and he didn't continue the practice, I ran into him several months later and he was able to paint and cycle again. He said he'd found a meditation that was helping him. I like to believe the Reiki sparked his healing.

Prepare: Sit quietly, upright, with feet planted on the floor. Touch the tip of your tongue to the roof of your mouth and focus on breathing deeply and evenly. Do this a few times to ground and center yourself. Then close your eyes and ask for the White Light of Protection to surround you as you call to your higher self and guides for assistance.

You may write the name of an illness, especially if its genetic, or just "My DNA," then close your hands in prayer position and invoke "DNA Reiki" for three to five minutes. Do it once or continue as needed.

Why do we often try anything and everything for pain management or chronic health issues and yet nothing seems to work? The teachings of this Reiki hold that memory cells in trauma areas will retain the pain longer if the emotion attached to it remains strong. Over time, crystals form physically and mentally and harden until you're fortunate enough to find a therapy to dissipate them.

Crystalline Reiki will start the process of breaking down these crystals. You will need to do two separate 15-minute sessions on yourself or as needed.

Prepare: Sit quietly, upright, with feet planted on the floor. Touch the tip of your tongue to the roof of your mouth and start to focus on breathing deeply and evenly. Do this a few times to ground and center yourself. Then close your eyes and ask for the White Light of Protection to surround you as you call to your higher self and guides for assistance.

Write "Crystals in body" or "Crystals in my [name body part here]" in your palm, then close your hands in prayer position and invoke for "Crystalline Reiki" for 15 minutes. This is the only technique you cannot perform remotely. Either place your hands on your client's shoulders, over the pain area, or do the hand practice with your client in front of you.

Try to experiment with different tools.

For instance, drug addiction or the long-term use of strong medication will build up crystals, too. So write "Crystals of [name of drug here]" in your hand, put your hands in prayer position, and invoke for Crystalline Reiki.

Another sticky topic for people is past lives. Some might argue, "What's the point of believing if we can't remember any of them in this life?" But a different question to consider is "What if?" What if you seem to never hold on to money long enough to be successful and it is due to past lives of poverty or of stealing from others? What if you can't stay in a relationship or always seem to be alone and friendless because in a past life you vowed chastity or had pushed people away all the time and these strong emotional

Lisa Okochi

behaviors or vows held energetic residues that continue to affect you now?

Past-life Reiki can help weaken the energy of negative residues.

Prepare: Sit quietly, upright, with feet planted on the floor. Touch the tip of your tongue to the roof of your mouth and start to focus on breathing deeply and evenly. Do this a few times to ground and center yourself. Then close your eyes and ask for the White Light of Protection to surround you as you call to your higher self and guides for assistance. Write "past life," or you might add "past life and [a theme, such as poverty]," in your hand, close your hands in prayer position, and invoke for "past-life Reiki" for three to five minutes.

Three invocations of past-life Reiki are probably enough, but feel free to perform more as needed.

I remember a story from a past-life-regression book about a severely overweight woman who tried everything to lose weight but nothing worked. She had a session and found out that long ago she was a very beautiful woman but was very nasty to anyone who was heavy. Yes, there is a theme of karma too. But consider the hours of unsuccessful therapy and treatments you may have gone through when your problems could very well stem from the residues of past lives. I would experiment with this important Reiki tool to address this possibility.

This next practice is similar to the karmic cords explained in Level 1. As there are karmic "cords" between people, there are some cords that can be negatively tying you down to a place you'd rather not be in but can't seem to pull away from. What if an alcoholic loved one always ended up going to the same liquor store or bar no matter how he might yearn to give up drinking? Reiki can help clear the temptations of a location that does not serve your well-being.

I once knew a person who wanted to stay in his childhood neighborhood but purposely moved away as far as possible because, as a recovering drug addict, it made him feel the pull of temptation. His present neighborhood probably has its pickup spots, but because he doesn't know where they are or go looking for them, he's OK. The same applies if you move away and can't stop missing your former workplace or home.

This next tool is a great way to help you detach from a negative location.

How to Detach from a Place Using Location Reiki

Prepare: Sit quietly, upright, with feet planted on the floor. Touch the tip of your tongue to the roof of your mouth and focus on breathing deeply and evenly. Do this a few times to ground and center yourself. Then close your eyes and ask for the White Light of Protection to surround you as you call to your higher self and guides for assistance. Write the name of the place, city, or country on your hand, then close your hands in prayer position and invoke "Location Reiki" for three to five minutes. Perform as often as needed.

If handling a client, write "For Tom Smith at [Tom's address] and his cords to [location]" in your palm or on a piece of paper, then close your hands in prayer position and invoke "Location Reiki."

There is one other simple practice that helps regulate your energy field when you feel "off." It is called the balance mudra, in which you "tent" your fingers in front of your chest or on your lap by having each fingertip lightly pressed against its counterpart, then invoke for "balance" for 30 seconds. In yogic mudras, each finger corresponds to an organ. That may explain why we feel balanced after this technique.

It's possible you'll feel a subtle energy flow up and down your body. The process will continue for about an hour and can be very helpful just before a meeting or something you need to focus on, like a delicate situation or important call.

There is one more useful K.R. tool that can help give you more energy: attuning objects. You can channel Reiki into personal belongings to use as protection or to enhance your vibration. Have you ever had a tie or color that you personally believed gave you luck, so you would wear it to an important interview or date? It's likely that you once wore it during a special event in your life and unconsciously empowered it with bringing you success or happiness. Your strong belief that it helped you succeed made its energy strong. As a Kundalini Reiki Master, you can now transfer Reiki to objects so they can help protect you or assist in your healing.

For example, tune your favorite pendant, crystal, ring, or watch to Reiki by placing it in your hands and invoking, "I ask my higher self to attune this [object] to Diamond Reiki" for 30 seconds. Then program it to protect you.

You will now be empowered to use all the tools from K.R. 1–3 to fully create shifts and changes in your life and situations and discover what you truly want. You may feel and act on the desire to lead a healthier lifestyle, to treat people better, or to solve problems with more clarity.

When you have adjusted to this frequency, it is recommended that you continue to the Gold Reiki and learn how it can consolidate your progress.

Case Studies

Client K.M. was on a flight from Los Angeles to New York when mid-flight the passenger next to her started to complain of intense menstrual pain and asked her if she had any Tylenol. Since the client did not have any, she decided to help her with K.R. After asking for permission, she sent the passenger a five-minute K.R. The client felt her hands get very hot and she "saw" white light pour down over the passenger. After 30 minutes, the passenger's pain had completely disappeared.

Client L. remotely sent Diamond Reiki from the U.S.A. to a very dear friend in Switzerland. The next day the friend e-mailed to say that she had felt very calm and peaceful ever since.

During a past-life Reiki practice in class, Client J. said she had a vision of herself as a prostitute who stole money from her clients. She said it made sense to her because all her boyfriends have always stolen from her!

In a class practice of past-life Reiki, Client S. said she had a vision of herself committing adultery many times in a previous life. She said it has helped her to understand why she is always attracted to married men!

CHAPTER 6

For Clients: Important Notes to Remember

This is a healing modality that may bring deep life issues to the surface. Although you are in a safe and protected environment, if at any time you feel you don't want to proceed, please feel free to let the K.R. Master know *before* the attunement starts—and leave quietly if there are others present.

Invoke for protection and assistance from whatever source you believe in to make the attunement powerful for you. You can call upon as many higher beings as you want, even the universe. Learn to ask your higher self for permission to get an attunement right before you start invoking and mentally hear your mind say "Yes." This will help you prepare to be quiet and still receive Reiki.

The level or power of each attunement will *always* be in accordance with how much each individual can handle. Don't expect to have the same experience as others in the group. There is a tendency for similar sensations, but it may be different for each individual.

As Reiki initially wants to clear your chakra blockages, your body may go through physical or emotional detox. Again, it will depend on your spiritual level and diet, among other things. After-effects sometimes noticed in the first three levels include: itchy sensations in the back of the throat, stomachache or gastric discomfort, diarrhea, nausea (this usually after Reiki 1 or 2 and only once), flu-like symptoms, headaches, light-headedness, and lethargy (especially after Reiki 3). All symptoms will eventually disappear as you practice the exercises in between levels and drink plenty of water.

Some have noticed they go through about a week of being short-tempered and nasty. This is also a type of mental and emotional detox, particularly if you are the type to hold in your real thoughts. But this too is usually just another phase of detoxing. Observe yourself carefully in these moments.

As your physical, gross energy adjusts to the higher, subtle frequencies, you will notice a lightness of being, focus, and clarity in your thoughts—depending on how often you keep up the practices. This is where the biggest differences arise as members compare progress.

It's one thing to be attuned to Kundalini Reiki, and it's quite another to actually start a full transition that will turn your life around.

After Reiki 3, you will be certified by the Kundalini Reiki Master to pass on the Reiki attunements.

CHAPTER 7

For Kundalini Reiki Practitioners

Once you are certified to attune, it might be difficult to accept that you can really pass on the K.R. attunements. Can it be so simple? *To attune or not to attune* becomes a dilemma. This is a personal decision and depends on your level of confidence. You will initially need to be supervised by your practitioner. Having said that, the following guidelines are suggested:

1. Leave at least five days between attunements to allow frequencies to absorb, especially as you detoxify.
2. Work on yourself first by practicing the exercises, especially your DNA, Birth-Trauma, Location, Crystalline, and Past-Life Reikis.
3. Get Reiki insurance and, if possible, C.P.R. certification. This is not required but is highly suggested, particularly if you are planning to rent space.

4. Start a healthy lifestyle, be well rested, meditate, and clear yourself a few minutes before you give an attunement. Follow the preparations diligently.

5. Never give an attunement when you are tired or, of course, dealing with a serious illness. When your defense system is low, you are more likely to be drained after attuning, which can take a couple of days to recover from.

<u>Very Important!</u>

Protecting Yourself and Your Client

We are dealing with energy. Yes, Reiki is a pure light source, so it cannot harm you. But there are other sources around that can be negative. So, before you begin your attunement, and to ensure that it is successful, clear the location with "Space-Clearing Reiki." Invoke for a protective shield of white light to surround yourself and the clients and say, "For no negative influences to interfere." This is another reason to invoke for your higher guides.

Make it a habit to have your client ask his or her higher self for permission to be attuned. Clients have remarked that it helped them be prepared.

For Reiki 1, ask again if the client wants to proceed. Sometimes, he or she may be getting nervous or scared. If the client decides to stop, and if you haven't paid for rental space, provide a refund. However, if the same client tries again and backs out a second time, do not.

As the Kundalini Reiki Master, you will be energetically connected to the client during the session. The client is attaching cords to your energetic field. Imagine how powerful it is when you are giving attunements to a group!

Before you call in the Reiki, give yourself a few minutes to ground your feet to the Earth, breathe deeply, and center yourself.

After the attunement, instruct the client to relax and allow the energy to absorb while you cut the cords between you. Then go and wash your hands.

How to Cut Cords to Disconnect

Mentally say "Cut!" and move your hand in a "slicing or axing" motion in front of your body a few times; wash your hands afterwards. Cutting cords applies to distant healing and attunements as well.

When you return, tell the client to sit up slowly and, as you wait, continue to re-center yourself. It is effective to pair up clients and have them share their experiences. You will likely overhear interesting reactions to comment on in open Q&A time.

You might feel somewhat drained later or the next day and realize that you forgot to either protect yourself or to cut the cords. Do it as soon as you remember. If you are the sensitive type, you might need to occasionally "sage" yourself with incense or take a salt bath.

Make sure to tell the client that he or she is in a safe and protected place and that any sensations will be entirely safe to feel.

Respect what anyone says and allow those who have knowledge to share insight—but be sure to maintain your leadership as their guide. You will likely have people who are masters of other healing modalities. Be respectful of them and suggest that this Reiki can enhance their skills. I am well trained in other types of healing but find this Reiki enhances them. Since all modalities are to heal, we can use the intention of Reiki to help intensify other therapies. Therapists say their clients are calmer when they invoke for them to be receptive before they arrive.

We Do Not Encourage Anyone to Stop Medications!

Although I have clients who managed to stop taking antidepressants or pain-management pills because of Kundalini Reiki, they did so at their own discretion. But having taken various precautions for some clients, it is very fulfilling to hear their many testimonials of pain relief, better focus, and the return of proper sleep.

To charge or not to charge is, again, a subjective dilemma. Isn't energy free? Founder Ole Gabrielsen answers that with a definitive yes, the energy itself is free and is not to be charged for, but you *do* charge for your time, in preparations, marketing, rentals, and the like, at your discretion. You might notice that if you do attune for free, the client will tend not to practice or appreciate this gift fully.

Try to charge at a rate that is reasonable and accessible to the community. Because this technique can help so many, it should be available to all classes.

I love this Reiki for its simplicity. I keep it simple so people from all walks of life feel they can do it too. I do notice deeper questions arise from those who pursue it at higher levels. You may suggest readings or videos as well. It is also suggested not to overwhelm clients who are very educated in spiritual and scientific fields with information overload.

At the same time, we are all individuals with different "flavors," so it will be natural for K.R. Masters to add their own style to healing attuning, but please keep to the base protocol until you have enough experience to shift it in any major way. Although the highest Reiki series in Ole Gabrielsen's attunements are the Ethereal Crystal levels, it is not recommended to attune clients only to this. The core power is to activate the Kundalini and to build on this foundation. To skip directly to higher levels of energy is like teaching a beginning guitarist complex melodies without providing the basic tools of chords and rhythm.

Most important is to insist that everyone practice, practice, practice!

If you practice healing often, you will occasionally need to "recharge your batteries" by attuning yourself as needed. Since we live in a society in which we are continually interacting with people, it is important to occasionally re-attune ourselves to keep our chakras clear.

How to Re-Attune Yourself or Self-Attune

While you can re-attune yourself as needed to keep your energy strong, over time you may notice that it no longer feels as powerful as it did. But this is more likely because your vibration has increased and not because the Reiki has weakened. This can be discouraging and lead to laziness, similar to the plateaus reached in a diet. Keep up your practice, however, and you will attain a never-ending level of enlightenment.

Step 1: Either purchase the Reiki Clinic exclusive audio from kundalinireiki.org or request it on Facebook, at Kundalini Reiki NYC, or attune a CD of calming music to K.R. for 30 seconds.

Step 2: Prepare. Sit quietly, upright, with feet planted on the floor. Touch the tip of your tongue to the roof of your mouth and focus on breathing deeply and evenly. Do this a few times to ground and center yourself. Then close your eyes and ask for the White Light of Protection to surround you as you call to your higher self and guides for assistance.

Step 3: Invoke. Call forth your guides and mentally say, "Please re-attune me to K.R. Level [number]." Do one level per re-attunement.

It is strongly suggested that you self-attune at least once a month to maintain your connection to the high frequencies. Even though the frequencies are permanently stored in your system, your energy field will not get congested with life issues. You don't even need to do the levels in the right order. Use your intuition to see which type is calling you. For instance, if you find yourself upset, re-attune to Gold Reiki Level and you will feel lighter and peaceful.

CHAPTER 8

Gold Reiki Attunements, Levels 1–3

This chapter will help you understand how Gold Reiki is different from K.R. and why it is recommended for you to receive this energy, too. There are countless frequencies in the higher realms, and other Reiki levels will bring your frequency closer to other dimensional vibrations as each level attunes you to more and more subtle energies, which will further help clear and strengthen your energy centers, leading to a focused, balanced, and happy life. We start truly delving into the metaphysical world. Gold Reiki is a different frequency from Kundalini Reiki and can be taken before Kundalini Reiki. However, it is suggested that you take Kundalini Reiki Levels 1–3 first and clear your energy fields to fully appreciate the power of Gold Reiki. This Reiki has two components: Gold Light and Golden Light Source.

If we try to define the differences between Kundalini and Gold Reiki, we can say that the K.R. levels help bring our biochemical, bioelectrical systems and physical, gross matter into alignment with the energy of our Mother Earth. By awakening our Kundalini, we are able to be completely grounded and "in" our bodies. Most of us are not in synch with our Kundalini Life Force, hence our foundations and survival instincts are weak. We are not living through our hearts, and our minds are struggling to avoid our bodies' physical and emotional needs. When we are "in" our bodies, we *want* to exercise, eat well, rest adequately, and have healthy relationships and lifestyles.

Gold Reiki reconnects us to our higher self—the spiritual aspect of our being that holds our true happiness and divine inner wisdom. Gold is the highest ray that is able to reach and connect to our human gross energy. It is extremely pure, and the quality is light, loving, and peaceful. It is a soft energy that makes you feel alert and alive.

Gold Reiki opens our heart centers to help us feel the soft warmth of unconditional love. The Golden Light frequency awakens joy and peace in our hearts. It removes the darkness and lower aspects, such as fear, and transmutes these into light. It dissipates negativity and pushes out hostility from others. When we feel our hearts open, we remember to feel gratitude. The frequency of gratitude attracts prosperity and abundance. In science, the electromagnetic amplitude of the heart is 60 times stronger than that of the brain. The heart can create miracles; the brain, mind power!

The Golden Source Reiki is the energy of "Christ Consciousness," where there is no duality. Black and white, right and wrong, all become meaningless as your self-awareness lets you acknowledge the unity of all experiences, beings with nature, and the Om of Absolute Truth. The Supreme God is one within you. It can help you see that bad experiences also teach you to grow.

Golden Source Reiki helps connect you to your higher self and inner wisdom, and clarifies your life purpose. It focuses more on your heart energy to reconnect you to unconditional love.

Attunements for Gold Reiki Levels 1–3

The preparations are the same for Gold 1–3 as for Kundalini Reiki 1–3, except that when you invoke, you ask to be attuned to Gold Reiki Level 1 and then 2, then to the Gold Source Reiki 3. There are no new tools to practice afterwards but to fine-tune the tools and exercises provided in K.R. Levels 1–3.

1. If you are not in a class, find a quiet space where you will not be disturbed for 30 minutes and turn off your cell phone. You may play calming music on a stereo, but do not wear headphones.
2. Sit in a comfortable position with palms facing upwards on your lap and legs flat on the floor. You may also lie down with your palms facing upwards. Do not cross your legs. This will allow for the Reiki to flow to your hand and feet chakras.
3. Touch the tip of your tongue to the roof of your mouth, center yourself with your breath, take three deep inhales into your heart, and exhale slowly. Take three breaths into your stomach to relax tension. Then invoke to your higher self and any guides or angels you believe in to ask for assistance and for the White Light of Protection to surround you. In your heart say, "Please attune me to Gold Reiki Level 1." Remember: for G.R. 3, we invoke to be attuned to the Golden Light Source.
4. Relax and allow the practitioner to channel the energy into your energy field.

The K.R. practitioner will connect you to the Reiki. It takes approximately 25 minutes for the K.R. Master to "download" the K.R. frequency into your energy field. All you need to do during the attunement is relax. If it is a private session, the K.R. Master will either sit near you or place his or her hands lightly on your shoulders. It is all right to fall asleep. Do not try to think too hard.

The Practice

The frequency of Gold Reiki is soft, calming, and loving. As you practice with the tools from KR 1–3, you can choose to invoke for G.R. instead.

For example, if you have a stomachache from something you ate, invoke for Kundalini Reiki. But if you have a stomachache from stress or anxiety, invoke for Gold Reiki.

Gold Reiki is very useful to send to ill clients and a family member in a stressful situation. It will calm them in periods of anxiety, pain, and fear. Learn to use your intuition to discern whether an issue is physical or more psychological, and apply a Reiki tool. Whatever you choose will not be a wrong choice. It's your intention that is important!

You can attune others to Gold Reiki after you complete Gold Reiki Level 3.

Case Studies

Client F.Z. had an elderly dog that had not been able to walk for sometime and was dying. After F.Z. gave it a few minutes of Gold Reiki, however, the dog managed to get up and walk towards her. Following a few more short Gold Reiki healings for her dog, the animal quietly and peacefully passed away. She strongly believes the Reiki helped her dog.

Client P.S. remotely sent Gold Reiki to a friend who was experiencing tremendous trouble with a family member. She said the next day the friend called her to let her know the family member had suddenly changed his mind for the better regarding a very bad situation. The short healing helped solve a difficult issue.

Client M.K. was trying to help her mother in Canada to recover from a bad chest cold and sent her Gold Reiki remotely. Her mother said she felt and "saw" golden light pour down her and into her chest, and she felt much better.

CHAPTER 9

Ethereal Crystal Reiki Attunements, Levels 1–9

This chapter will help you understand why crystals are commonly used in healing, what Ethereal Crystals are, and how they can further empower your Reiki abilities.

Before we contemplate the meaning of Ethereal Crystals, let us first discuss physical crystals. Crystals are minerals formed in Mother Nature. They have energetic healing qualities. It is scientifically agreed that everything in life is made of energy. Whether animate or inanimate, everything has its own unique vibration. Just as the energy of the food we choose to eat can be either nutritious, invoke feelings of comfort, or cause allergies or highs and lows, crystals also have properties that affect our moods and energetic systems at deep levels. Quartz crystals, for example, have similar properties as our bodies at a cellular level, so they resonate well and can help shift and balance us as we hold, wear, or place them near us.

Each crystal emits unique vibrations that bring out certain qualities we want to enhance or clear. At the same time, there are a few contraindications. For instance, amethysts help hone our spirituality, intellectual focus, and attract lucid dreaming, but the stones are contraindicated for cancer. Amethyst has the vibration that can potentially encourage the growth of cancer cells. In addition, we must remember that energy waves do not vibrate in one direction; we are also affecting the crystals, so crystals need to be recharged and cleaned regularly as they absorb our energetic blockages. On the other hand, once a crystal balances out a specific issue, it will then magnify the attribute you desire and raise your vibration. Rose quartz, for instance, will enhance feelings of unconditional love and, in turn, attract love from others because you are emitting that frequency.

In the world of spirituality and alternative therapy, crystals are also associated with chakras and are used for clearing energy blockages, healing, and stimulation. Each crystal corresponds to certain chakras depending on their qualities (including, sometimes, color) and are placed either directly over chakras or on the area causing discomfort. This manual is not intended to go into detail over every usage and meaning of crystals, but the following are most common:

Clear quartz is the most versatile and safe crystal to use when in doubt.

Black tourmaline is very good for protection from negativity, toxic situations, and the like.

Rosa quartz represents unconditional love and is good for the heart chakra.

Amethyst is used for focus ands spirituality.

Tiger eye is for grounding and confidence, for use on the base or solar-plexus chakra.

You can also choose a crystal based on its color and associate it to the color of a chakra:

Root: Red

Sacral: Orange

Solar plexus: Yellow

Heart: Green or pink

Throat: Blue

Third Eye: Magenta

Crown: White and purple

Throat: Blue

Ethereal Crystals and Their Uses

The *Merriam-Webster's* dictionary defines "ethereal" as: "of or relating to regions beyond the earth; spiritual; intangible." Ethereal Crystals are obtained from creating or calling forth the spiritual and healing properties of crystals from the spiritual realms and deep down from the "crystalline core" of Gaia, Mother Earth, where powerful gemstones are said to be stored. The "ethereal" energy from these crystals is 400 percent stronger and can be used to either strengthen your physical crystals or replace them when healing. Although it is possible to meditate and use intentions to create them, it is far easier and powerful to be attuned to their frequencies by an E.C.R. practitioner. When you are attuned, the frequencies of crystals are permanently stored in your system, so you can call upon them within seconds!

There are nine levels, and the attunements follow the same preparations and tools as for K.R. This concept may be somewhat difficult to grasp as it involves how to call forth crystal frequencies of spiritual crystals. For example:

1. Learning how to apply the frequencies of an amethyst to help heal or strengthen an attunement.
2. How to "place" Ethereal Crystals on certain chakras to expedite a healing session.
3. How to energize water with Ethereal Crystals to up to 400 percent of its energy.

Ethereal Crystal Levels 1–3 Attunements: Preparing for the Attunements and the Crystals That You Will Receive

There are nine levels to Ethereal Crystals, and the prerequisites are Kundalini Reiki 1, 2 and 3. The attunements will be covered in three sessions (1–3, 4–6, and 7–9) but can be done individually if one is relatively new to Reiki.

Ethereal Crystal Levels 1–3 will attune you to the following crystals:

Crystal	Qualities	Benefits
amber	Warm	Clarity
amethyst	Spiritual, 7th ch.	Protection
aquamarine	4th,5th chakra	Communication
aventurine	Gold stone	Sunny, light
pink Beryl	4th chakra	Divine Love
blue lace agate	5th chakra	Confidence
Botswana agate	Adapt to change	Central nervous system
green calcite	Prosperity	Business
Carnelian	1st,2nd,3rd chakra	Creativity, sexaul
Chrysocolla	5th chakra	Intuition
Citrine	Happy, warm	Manifest
clear quartz	Amplify	Programmability
Diamond	7th chakra, stregth	Truth, clarity
single terminated clear quartz	Clarity	Focus, intention
Emerald	4th chakra	Healing, love
Hematite	1st chakra	Ground, protect
red jasper	1st,2nd chakra	Vitality
Malachite	Heart healing	Confidence
rose quartz	4th chakra	Unconditional love
Ruby	Root chakra	Passion, ground
Solidite	3rd eye	Intuition
Turquoise	Wisdom	Protection

Preparations

1. If you are not in a class, find a quiet space where you will not be disturbed for 30 minutes and turn off your cell phone. You may play calming music on a stereo, but do not wear headphones.
2. Sit in a comfortable position with palms facing upwards on your lap and legs flat on the floor. You may also lie down with your palms facing upwards. Do not cross your legs. This will allow for the Reiki to flow to your hand and feet chakras.
3. Touch the tip of your tongue to the roof of your mouth, center yourself with your breath, take three deep inhales into your heart, and exhale slowly. Take three breaths into your stomach to relax tension. Then invoke to your higher self and any guides or angels you believe in to ask for assistance and for the White Light of Protection to surround you. In your heart say, "Please attune me to Ethereal Crystal Reiki Level 1–3."
4. Relax and allow the E.C.R. practitioner to channel the energy into your energy field.

The E.C.R. practitioner will connect you to the Reiki. It takes approximately 25 minutes for the E.C.R. Master to "download" the frequency into your energy field. All you need to do during the attunement is relax. If it is a private session, the practitioner will either sit near you or place his or her hands lightly on your shoulders. It is all right to fall asleep. Do not try to think too hard.

Ethereal Crystals of Levels 4–6

Crystal	Qualities	Benefits
Alexandrite	Changes Color	Adapting
Amazonite	Truth	Hope, integrity
Azurite	Sacred	Awakening
Bloodstone	Detoxing	Fires energy
Gold calcite	3rd eye	Meditation
Fire opal	Magical	Luck
Fluorite	Order of chaos	Perspective
Red garnet	Cures	Protect, intensity
Jade	Longevity	Luck, courage
Lapis lazuri	5th chakra	Awareness
Moldavite	Outer space	Ethereal spirit
Moonstone	Destiny	Hormones
Peridot	Arch A Raphael	Healing Heart
Pyrite	Money symbol	Poverty conscious
Blue sapphire	5th chakra	Creativity
Yellow sapphire	Warm	Attract Wealth
Black tourmaline	1st chakra	Purifies, protects
Violet tourmaline	6th chakra	Spirit
Pink tourmaline	4th chakra	Self love
Double terminated clear quartz	Amplifier of intentions	Clarity

Preparations

1. If you are not in a class, find a quiet space where you will not be disturbed for 30 minutes and turn off your cell phone. You may play calming music on a stereo, but do not wear headphones.
2. Sit in a comfortable position with palms facing upwards on your lap and legs flat on the floor. You may also lie down with your palms facing upwards. Do not cross your legs. This will allow for the Reiki to flow to your hand and feet chakras.
3. Touch the tip of your tongue to the roof of your mouth, center yourself with your breath, take three deep inhales into your heart, and exhale slowly. Take three breaths into your stomach to relax tension. Then invoke to your higher self, Master Kuthumi, and any guides or angels you believe in to ask for assistance and for the White Light of Protection to surround you. In your heart say, "Please attune me to Ethereal Crystal Reiki Level 4–6."
4. Relax and allow the E.C.R. practitioner to channel the energy into your energy field.

The E.C.R. practitioner will connect you to the Reiki. It takes approximately 25 minutes for the E.C.R. Master to "download" the frequency into your energy field. All you need to do during the attunement is relax. If it is a private session, the practitioner will either sit near you or place his or her hands lightly on your shoulders. It is all right to fall asleep.

Ethereal Crystals of Levels 7–9

Crystal	Qualities	Benefits
Chariot	Spiritual growth	Entity release
Sugulith	Healer stone	Shock/dissapoint
Rhodochrost	Love	Balance
Pyritsun	Healer's gold	
Prasm (African jade)	Ancient	Attracts love
Snowflake	Soothes	Sacral, power
Obsidian	Volcanic crystal	Fear, anger
Apache tears	Obsidian	Power
Moon marbles		
Boji stones		Arthritis, back pain
Tektite	Energy	Strengthen aura
Chalcedon	Miracle	Depression
Larimar (Atlantis stone)	Throat chakra	Freedom
Labordorite	Protection	De stresses
Kunzite	Love healing	Broken heart
Heliotrop	Blood stone	Blood cleansing
Cyanite	Psychic	Calms mind
Apophylite	3rd eye	Meditation
Ruby-zoisite	Transmutes neg	Lethargy, stamina

Ethereal Crystal Levels 7–9 will attune you to the following:

Preparations

1. If you are not in a class, find a quiet space where you will not be disturbed for 30 minutes and turn off your cell phone. You may play calming music on a stereo, but do not wear headphones.
2. Sit in a comfortable position with palms facing upwards on your lap and legs flat on the floor. You may also lie down with your palms facing upwards. Do not cross your legs. This will allow for the Reiki to flow to your hand and feet chakras.
3. Touch the tip of your tongue to the roof of your mouth, center yourself with your breath, take three deep inhales into your heart, and exhale slowly. Take three breaths into your stomach to relax tension. Then invoke to your higher self, Master Kuthumi, and any guides or angels you believe in to ask for assistance and for the White Light of Protection to surround you. In your heart say, "Please attune me to Ethereal Crystal Reiki Level 6–9."
4. Relax and allow the E.C.R. practitioner to channel the energy into your energy field.

The E.C.R. practitioner will connect you to the Reiki. It takes approximately 25 minutes for the E.C.R. Master to "download" the frequency into your energy field. All you need to do during the attunement is relax. If it is a private session, the practitioner will either sit near you or place his or her hands lightly on your shoulders.

The Practices for E.C.R. Levels 1–9

How to Use This Energy to Facilitate Healings

1. Create a Gem Elixir

You can start using this tool to create gem elixirs after E.C.R. Attunement Level 3. Ethereal crystals are said to be 400 percent stronger than physical ones. You can now empower medication, supplements, facial products, water, and other things with E.C.R. to make them more effective. You can research the healing qualities of a specific crystal from the attunements and invoke for its energy to enhance the benefits of a product.

For example, place a bottle of medicine with the cap off in your hands and cup it. Invoke for spiritual assistance. Mentally say, "Place an amethyst crystal in this medicine." When in doubt, simply say, "Ethereal Crystal Reiki!" It will be charged in 30 seconds.

You may also place a glass of water in front of you. Mentally say, "Place [name of Ethereal Crystal] in water!" The water will be charged in 30 seconds.

2. Strengthen a Real Crystal with E.C.R.

If you have real crystals and/or wear them, you can enhance their power with E.C.R. Invoke for spiritual assistance, put the stone in your hands, and mentally say, "Place [name of Ethereal Crystal] in [your stone]." Your stone will be strengthened in seconds.

When you give a regular healing, you can place E.C.R. attuned crystals or just the Ethereal Crystals on the client's chakras. If you are using E.C.'s, then simply point to a client's chakra, mentally invoke, and say, "Place a [name of crystal] here!" You can also give a self-healing using the same technique.

Using crystals in a healing session: A protocol for chakra balancing using real or ethereal crystals.

Base chakra: Ruby. Ignites enthusiasm and courage, drives away sadness and depression. Good for adrenals, circulation, and protection.

Sacral chakra: Carnelian. Encourages spirit of community and life's emotions, and dispels apathy. Good for rheumatism, arthritis, neuralgia, infertility, depression.

Solar-plexus chakra: Amber. Encourages sunny nature, self-confidence. Helps stomach, spleen, liver, gallbladder.

Heart chakra: Rose quartz. Gentleness, openness, kindness, sensitivity, and empathy. Calms stress and encourages the development of unconditional love.

Throat chakra: Turquoise. Inner calm, communication, creativity. Helps viral infection, acts as an anti-inflammatory, and relaxes cramps. It is a powerful booster for the whole anatomy and fosters nutrient absorption.

Third Eye chakra: Lapis lazuli. For inner wisdom and honesty. Reveals own inner truth, helps open awareness and widen knowledge of ancient wisdom.

Crown chakra: Amethyst. Spiritual awakening and inner peace. Promotes understanding of the unity of all life with the Om—the oneness.

Preparations

1. Touch the tip of your tongue to the roof of your mouth, center yourself with your breath, take three deep inhales into your heart, and exhale slowly. Take

three breaths into your stomach to relax tension. Then invoke to your higher self and any guides or angels you believe in to ask for assistance and for the White Light of Protection to surround you. Say, "Please place [name of crystal] on this client's [chakra]. Ethereal Crystal Reiki!"

2. Simply point to or touch the body location and mentally say the name of the stone you want to put there. The crystal energy will stay there and then disappear when it's no longer needed. You can also mentally point to and place a stone on an organ.

For example, place a citrine on the bladder.

Place Ethereal Crystals on chakras as a healing session or add on to a massage or aromatherapy session. The best part is they don't fall off like real stones!

When you are not sure: Just ask Kuthumi to place the right crystals where needed and invoke "Ethereal Crystal Reiki."

You can also invoke for one particular crystal and add it on to a Kundalini Reiki invocation.

For example, invoke and mentally say, "Kundalini Reiki with ethereal amethyst crystal!" and visualize its energy pouring down your body.

CHAPTER 10

How to Heal and Attune Remotely: An Overview

While this manual is intended primarily for K.R. practitioners, the beauty of it is that it can be used by a layman after a certain amount of supervision and practice. But please note that every one of these practices should be performed only after the completion of each level. All masters of other healing modalities must be attuned to this updated version.

Part 1: Healing Someone Remotely

You can start healing loved ones in other cities or countries as you finish each level.

Preparations

First ask for permission. Not everyone will agree to healings. Then arrange a time where you both can be in a quiet place for a few minutes. You can also tell the person prior to healing to sit and relax, and, later, to allow the healing to absorb following the five-minute healing session. Ask the receiver to prepare as you did before the agreed time, instruct him or her to relax, and focus on the issue to alleviate. You can also invoke for spiritual assistance.

The steps are similar to the self-healing practices. Both of you should sit in a comfortable position, with palms facing upwards on your lap, legs flat on the floor, or lie down, with your palms facing upwards. Do not cross your legs. This will allow the Reiki to flow to your hand and feet chakras.

1. Touch the tip of your tongue to the roof of your mouth, center yourself with your breath, take three deep inhales into your heart, and exhale slowly. Take three breaths into your stomach to relax tension. Then invoke to your higher self, Master Kuthumi, and any guides or angels you believe in to ask for assistance for the White Light of Protection to surround you.

2. Write the person's name and address in your hand, invoke, and ask for whatever issues to clear for the receiver. For example, "I ask for God, my spirit guide, and Master Kuthumi to assist me in sending healing to Tom Smith at 222 Street, Chicago, Illinois, for his asthma. Kundalini Reiki!" If, for instance, the receiver is going through a difficult divorce, you might say, "I ask for my God, spirit guides, and Master Kuthumi to assist me in sending healing to Tom Smith at 222 Street, Chicago, Illinois, for his divorce to go smoothly. Gold Reiki!"

3. When you're done, express thanks for the assistance and cut the cords between you and the receiver. You can arrange for a follow-up call or e-mail as needed.

Part 2: Attuning Someone Remotely

To attune someone in person or distantly requires more careful planning. Yes, you are certified to attune after completing each series, but you will need supervision and practice using the tools of self-healing before you commit. Make sure you are not feeling tired or unwell when attuning or your energy may get drained.

Preparations

Purchase this *Kundalini Reiki Manual* for your receiver or have the receiver purchase it online through iUniverse or Amazon. There are Kindle and Nook versions available, too, although having a physical copy will let you find different sections more easily. Have the receiver read the manual first and then each chapter that corresponds to the level you are attuning him to. This way, he will be aware of what to generally expect, especially possible detoxing.

Prepare the receiver just like you were prepared as the client. Review the preparation steps from each series.

1. Agree to a set time of 30 minutes during which you can both remain uninterrupted. Ask the receiver to play soft, calming music. Tell him to sit in a comfortable position, with palms facing upwards on his lap, legs flat on the floor, or to lay down with his palms facing upwards. Tell him not to cross his legs. This will allow the Reiki to flow to the hand and feet chakras. Have him read the chapter corresponding to the attunement that he will receive. Walk through the instructions if needed.

2. I suggest you purchase the exclusive K.R. clinic audio from kundalinireiki.org, request one on

Facebook (Kundalini Reiki NYC), or attune to a calming CD of Kundalini Reiki for 30 seconds. This way you can time the session.

3. You do *not* need to be conducting the attunement via FaceTime or phone. Both you and the receiver must invoke and ask for the selected attunement level. Invoke, for example, "Tom Smith [include address] to be attuned to K.R. Level 1." Make sure you write the full name and address of the receiver in your hand or on a piece of paper. Then relax with your hands in the prayer pose for 25 minutes and have total faith that the Reiki is attuning the receiver. Arrange for feedback about an hour afterward, allowing the receiver time to absorb the experience.

4. You must attune one level at a time and in proper order—except for E.C.R., which you attune to three levels at a time. For example, "Please attune Tom Smith at 222 Street, Chicago, Illinois, to Ethereal Crystal Reiki Levels 1–3."

Finish one series within three weeks. Do not leave more than one week in between during a series.

After you receive feedback, walk through the practices and help the receiver understand the tools. Please seek supervision from the K.R. practitioner until you are confident to perform the practice on your own.

Remember to disconnect after healings and attunements by cutting the cords with K.R., and try to re- attune yourself every now and then. Please review the practices until they become part of your daily routine. A K.R. or G.R. invocation is a great way to start your day, giving you focus, energy, and a sense of well-being.

CHAPTER 11

Reiki Clinic for the Community

Once you have acquired enough confidence and practice in the Reiki energy under the supervision of a K.R. practitioner, you might want to start offering hands-on healing sessions to your community. This more traditional approach may be your initial step to attract clients to attunements.

The following photos depict the various hand positions. You may, as a Reiki practitioner, already be familiar with them. Or you may know slightly different versions. Please ask your K.R. practitioner how to conduct a hands-on session. The basics are similar to traditional Reiki, but be sure to invoke for K.R., G.R., or whatever type of Reiki feels best for the client.

Note: Please go to <u>kundalinireiki.org</u> watch the Reiki clinic demo.

Kundalini Reiki Clinic Practitioners' Guidelines

During the healing, there will be a 30 min audio for timing. You will switch hands positions each time you hear 2 gongs, each time healing a different chakra.

There will be a total of 6 different hands positions as described below. We will have 1, 2 or 3 healers per patient. We also get to heal each other at the end! Please arrive@7:30pm for the brief.

Option 1	1 HEALER
Hands Position 1	Around Head
Hands Position 2	Third Eye & Eyes
Hands Position 3	Throat
Hands Position 4	Heart
Hands Position 5	Solar Plexus
Hands Position 6	Sacral

Option 2	1 HEALER NEXT TO THE HEAD	1 or 2 HEALERS BY PATIENT'S SIDE
Hands Position 1	Around Head	Heart
Hands Position 2	Third Eye & Eyes	Solar Plexus
Hands Position 3	Throat	Sacral
	Gently ask patient to lie on the belly	
Hands Position 4	Back of Head	Back of Navel (lower back)
Hands Position 5	Back of Heart	Ground / Base Chakra
Hands Position 6	Back of Solar Plexus	Feet

3ND EYE + EYES | AROUND HEAD | THROAT + JAW | BACK HEAD | BACK HEART

HEART MAN | HEART WOMAN raised hands | SOLAR PLEXUS | SACRAL CHAKRA | BACK SOLAR PLEXUS

KNEE + FEET | FEET | GROUND CHAKRA patient lie on belly | SHOULDERS | BACK NAVEL / LOWER BACK

Lisa Okochi

For example, you may start by placing your hands a few inches above the shoulders of a client, invoking for Master Kuthumi and other spirit guides to assist you, and saying, "Kundalini Reiki." Treat for 5–15 minutes or by working your way down the body in 5-minute increments.

You may also place your hands directly on a client's body, but please remember to keep the touch light. Clients will not feel comfortable if your hands are heavy or tremble. Some healers prefer hovering their hands above a client's body. It's up to you.

You can either follow the hand positions down the body or place your hands locally over the problem area. However, just placing your hands over a client's shoulders will be fine because the Kundalini Reiki will go to where it's needed most!

Please remember to invoke for protection before each client and "cut" the cords afterward between the two of you. This is extremely important, otherwise you will continue to be connected, and that may drain your energy! This manual is meant to be a guideline for anyone who wishes to begin helping others with Reiki.

CONCLUSION

A good way to start is by practicing on a pet—animals are very aware and sensitive to Reiki energy—or a family member or friend going through a stressful time. Practice at your workplace by invoking it to be a smooth, peaceful day or clear the energy of the office with "Location Reiki." If you start practicing Reiki on yourself, you will indirectly affect your home and family in positive ways. Try to be aware of how things might shift. Notice how people behave towards you as you practice.

You cannot use this Reiki for negative purposes as it is pure light. If someone tries, that negative force will come back to you a hundred-fold. It is the law of karma. So, treat this Reiki with loving care and respect. Know that whatever time and effort you put into practicing will reap results accordingly.

This manual is the recipe!

It is often pointed out that happiness cannot be found in money, the perfect job, or the ideal partner. For it is in human nature to find dissatisfaction again at some point. True happiness is the ability to take on challenges that call to you from your heart and to find fulfillment as you learn from them to become a better person. Find joy as well in little accomplishments. As the Reiki opens your heart, discover your true self and potential.

As we have progressed from the clunky computers of the 80s, so too has spirituality progressed. Alchemy is not as far-fetched an idea now as quantum physics was in discovering the potential depth of the universe, the theory of other dimensions, the breaking down of particles to nanoparticles to create tiny devices to advance medicine.

Science and spirituality are coming together to uncover the secrets to optimum health and, hopefully, happiness. Since you are reading this manual, you are probably searching for alternative ways to balance your lifestyle and promote well-being. You might be sensing yourself and others to be feeling heavy, stuck, or lacking in focus. If you are sleeping poorly, gaining weight for no clear reason, or losing short-term memory, it likely due to the planetary shifts and solar flares that have been intensifying since 2012. Major portals have opened and continue to bring down higher dimensional frequencies that can greatly affect every being on this planet as they adjust and try to merge into our own biochemical and bioelectrical fields.

So, practice this Kundalini Reiki and invoke for assistance from your heart to the spiritual universe.

I dedicate this manual to the founder, Ole Gabrielsen, for gifting me with his amazing Kundalini Reiki healing system, which has forever changed my own healing practice and teachings. It is now my mission to pass on the K.R. energy and practice to others so they may similarly improve their lives.

Namaste ("The divinity in me salutes the divinity in you").

KUNDALINI REIKI
QUICK REFERENCE
GUIDE

Attunement guide times.	Attunement type and level	What to think after the attunement to activate the Reiki with your intention.	What you can do after each attunement with the though intention and approximate treatment time.
Starting point	Kundalini Reiki 1	Reiki	Self healing - 5 minutes .
			Healing karmic bands
			Situation Healing
			Distant Healing
5 days after 1	Kundalini Reiki 2	Kundalini Reiki	All of the above
		Kundalini Reiki Meditation	Receive the daily meditation to cleanse your energy channels. 5 – 15.
10 days after 2	Kundalini Reiki 3 Master	As above	All of the above and attune others to this energy.
Balance	Place fingers and thumbs of opposing hands together for 30 seconds and you receive a full rebalancing of your energy systems over the next hour.		
Diamond Reiki	To pass the Reiki through an etheric diamond. 5 minutes		
Crystalline Reiki	Two hands-on healing sessions per person for dissolving the crystalline deposits left in the body from traumas. (both emotional and physical) 15 minutes * Use on yourself first		
DNA	For strengthening the ability to heal DNA strands and defects! 3 – 5 minutes Reiki *Use on yourself first		
Birth trauma Reiki	Healing the trauma of birth. 1 treatment per patient 3 – 5 minutes * Use on yourself first		
Location Reiki	For healing the bonds and ties we have with places. 1 treatment per person 3 – 5 minutes * Use on yourself first		
Past life	It takes three sessions to complete the treatment. 5 minutes or longer. Reiki * Use on yourself first		
5 days between all. Must have KR3 first.	Kundalini Reiki Boosters:	There are 6 extra levels of KR which fortify the KR1-3 and open your energy channels wider especially in the hands.	
5 days between all. Must have KR3 first.	Gold Reiki Levels1 to 3	Gold Reiki	Transmutes darkness into light, this works on a very high frequency of light.
5 days between all. Must have KR3 first.	Ethereal crystals Levels1 to 6	I place (name of crystal/s) into position in body or chakra.	Places an ethereal crystal inside the person to heal and balance etc.

SUGGESTED READING

Kundalini Reiki Manual, by Lisa Okochi. To be used as a textbook and guide for K.R. students and practitioners.

It Works, free e-book by R. H. Jarett.

The Game of Life, free e-book by Florence Scovel Shinn.

Emotional Wisdom, by Dina Saxer.

Wheels of Light: A Study of the Chakras, by Rosslyn Bruyere.

The Seed of Christ/Buddha Within You, by Simon Kim and Susanna Eun. A study of non-duality. Published by Createspace, Inc.

Free download for crystal qualities: crownjewels.com.

SUGGESTED VIDEOS

What the Bleep Do We Know?, by William Arntz.

What's Down the Rabbit Hole, by William Arntz.

Contact: Ole Gabrielsen at ole@olegabrielsen.com.

ABOUT THE AUTHOR

Lisa Okochi, NY LMT and NY Yoga Instructor. BA in Intercultural Communications from Tokyo ICU University in Japan.

Meditiation Guide who has been practicing energy work for many years. Currently Leader and Organizer of Kundalini Reiki teachings and Attunements in USA and other countries.

CONTACT: kundalinireiki.org
Facebook Kundalini reiki NYC

Printed in the United States
By Bookmasters